ALTO SAX

101 MOVIE HITS

Available for
FLUTE, CLARINET, ALTO SAX, TENOR SAX, TRUMPET,
HORN, TROMBONE, VIOLIN, VIOLA, CELLO

ISBN 978-1-4950-6065-6

HAL•LEONARD®
CORPORATION
7777 W. BLUEMOUND RD. P.O. BOX 13819 MILWAUKEE, WI 53213

Visit Hal Leonard Online at
www.halleonard.com

CONTENTS

AGAINST ALL ODDS
(Take a Look at Me Now)
from AGAINST ALL ODDS

ALTO SAX

Words and Music by
PHIL COLLINS

ALFIE

Theme from the Paramount Picture ALFIE

ALTO SAX

Words by HAL DAVID
Music by BURT BACHARACH

AXEL F

Theme from the Paramount Motion Picture BEVERLY HILLS COP

ALTO SAX

By HAROLD FALTERMEYER

BABY ELEPHANT WALK

from the Paramount Picture HATARI!

ALTO SAX

By HENRY MANCINI

BEAUTY AND THE BEAST

from Walt Disney's BEAUTY AND THE BEAST

ALTO SAX

Music by ALAN MENKEN
Lyrics by HOWARD ASHMAN

Moderately slow
To Coda
D.C. al Coda
CODA

BLAZE OF GLORY

featured in the film YOUNG GUNS II

ALTO SAX

Words and Music by
JON BON JOVI

BLUE VELVET

featured in the Motion Picture BLUE VELVET

ALTO SAX

Words and Music by BERNIE WAYNE
and LEE MORRIS

BORN FREE

from the Columbia Pictures' Release BORN FREE

ALTO SAX

Words by DON BLACK
Music by JOHN BARRY

CALL ME

from the Paramount Motion Picture AMERICAN GIGOLO

ALTO SAX

Words by DEBORAH HARRY
Music by GIORGIO MORODER

CAN YOU FEEL THE LOVE TONIGHT

from Walt Disney Pictures' THE LION KING

ALTO SAX

Music by ELTON JOHN
Lyrics by TIM RICE

CAN'T HELP FALLING IN LOVE

from the Paramount Picture BLUE HAWAII

ALTO SAX

Words and Music by GEORGE DAVID WEISS, HUGO PERETTI and LUIGI CREATORE

Moderately slow

THE CANDY MAN

from WILLY WONKA AND THE CHOCOLATE FACTORY

ALTO SAX

Words and Music by LESLIE BRICUSSE
and ANTHONY NEWLEY

CHARIOTS OF FIRE

from CHARIOTS OF FIRE

ALTO SAX

By VANGELIS

Moderately, majestically
1.
2.

COLORS OF THE WIND

from Walt Disney's POCAHONTAS

ALTO SAX

Music by ALAN MENKEN
Lyrics by STEPHEN SCHWARTZ

Moderately

D.S. al Coda
CODA

COME SATURDAY MORNING

(Saturday Morning)

from the Paramount Picture THE STERILE CUCKOO

ALTO SAX

Words by DORY PREVIN
Music by FRED KARLIN

CUPS
(When I'm Gone)
from the Motion Picture Soundtrack PITCH PERFECT

ALTO SAX

Words and Music by A.P. CARTER,
LUISA GERSTEIN and HELOISE TUNSTALL-BEHRENS

COME WHAT MAY

from the Motion Picture MOULIN ROUGE

ALTO SAX

Words and Music by
DAVID BAERWALD

DANGER ZONE

from the Motion Picture TOP GUN

ALTO SAX

Words and Music by GIORGIO MORODER
and TOM WHITLOCK

DEAR HEART

from DEAR HEART

ALTO SAX

Music by HENRY MANCINI
Words by JAY LIVINGSTON and RAY EVANS

DIAMONDS ARE A GIRL'S BEST FRIEND

from GENTLEMEN PREFER BLONDES

ALTO SAX

Words by LEO ROBIN
Music by JULE STYNE

DO YOU KNOW WHERE YOU'RE GOING TO?

Theme from MAHOGANY

ALTO SAX

Words by GERRY GOFFIN
Music by MICHAEL MASSER

DON'T YOU (FORGET ABOUT ME)

from the Universal Picture THE BREAKFAST CLUB

ALTO SAX

Words and Music by KEITH FORSEY
and STEVE SCHIFF

THE DREAME

from the film SENSE AND SENSIBILITY

ALTO SAX

By PATRICK DOYLE

END OF THE ROAD

from the Paramount Motion Picture BOOMERANG

ALTO SAX

Words and Music by BABYFACE, L.A. REID and DARYL SIMMONS

ENDLESS LOVE

from ENDLESS LOVE

ALTO SAX

Words and Music by
LIONEL RICHIE

EVERYBODY'S TALKIN'

(Echoes)

from MIDNIGHT COWBOY

ALTO SAX

Words and Music by
FRED NEIL

EXHALE

(Shoop Shoop)

from WAITING TO EXHALE

ALTO SAX

Words and Music by
BABYFACE

EYE OF THE TIGER

Theme from ROCKY III

ALTO SAX

Words and Music by FRANK SULLIVAN
and JIM PETERIK

FOOTLOOSE

Theme from the Paramount Motion Picture FOOTLOOSE

ALTO SAX

Words by DEAN PITCHFORD
Music by KENNY LOGGINS

Fast Rock

FORREST GUMP – MAIN TITLE

(Feather Theme)

from the Paramount Motion Picture FORREST GUMP

ALTO SAX

Music by ALAN SILVESTRI

HALLELUJAH

featured in the DreamWorks Motion Picture SHREK

ALTO SAX

Words and Music by
LEONARD COHEN

GLORY OF LOVE

Theme from KARATE KID PART II

ALTO SAX

Words and Music by DAVID FOSTER,
PETER CETERA and DIANE NINI

HAPPY

from DESPICABLE ME 2

ALTO SAX

Words and Music by
PHARRELL WILLIAMS

THE HEAT IS ON

from the Paramount Motion Picture BEVERLY HILLS COP

ALTO SAX

Words by KEITH FORSEY
Music by HAROLD FALTERMEYER

Moderately fast Rock

HELLO AGAIN

from the Motion Picture THE JAZZ SINGER

ALTO SAX

Words by NEIL DIAMOND
Music by NEIL DIAMOND
and ALAN LINDGREN

HOW DEEP IS YOUR LOVE

from the Motion Picture SATURDAY NIGHT FEVER

ALTO SAX

Words and Music by BARRY GIBB, ROBIN GIBB and MAURICE GIBB

I AM A MAN OF CONSTANT SORROW

featured in O BROTHER, WHERE ART THOU?

ALTO SAX

Words and Music by
CARTER STANLEY

I BELIEVE I CAN FLY

from SPACE JAM

ALTO SAX

Words and Music by
ROBERT KELLY

I JUST CALLED TO SAY I LOVE YOU

featured in THE WOMAN IN RED

ALTO SAX

Words and Music by
STEVIE WONDER

Moderately

I WILL ALWAYS LOVE YOU

featured in THE BODYGUARD

ALTO SAX

Words and Music by
DOLLY PARTON

Moderately slow
3
small notes optional

I WILL WAIT FOR YOU

from THE UMBRELLAS OF CHERBOURG

ALTO SAX

Music by MICHEL LEGRAND
Original French Text by JACQUES DEMY
English Words by NORMAN GIMBEL

(I'VE HAD) THE TIME OF MY LIFE

from DIRTY DANCING

ALTO SAX

Words and Music by FRANKE PREVITE,
JOHN DeNICOLA and DONALD MARKOWITZ

JAILHOUSE ROCK

from JAILHOUSE ROCK

ALTO SAX

Words and Music by JERRY LEIBER
and MIKE STOLLER

Moderately

THE JOHN DUNBAR THEME

from DANCES WITH WOLVES

ALTO SAX

By JOHN BARRY

KOKOMO

from the Motion Picture COCKTAIL

ALTO SAX

Words and Music by JOHN PHILLIPS,
TERRY MELCHER, MIKE LOVE,
and SCOTT McKENZIE

Moderately bright
To Coda
1.
2.
D.S. al Coda
CODA

LET THE RIVER RUN

Theme from the Motion Picture WORKING GIRL

ALTO SAX

Words and Music by
CARLY SIMON

LET IT GO

from Disney's Animated Feature FROZEN

ALTO SAX

Music and Lyrics by KRISTEN ANDERSON-LOPEZ
and ROBERT LOPEZ

Fine
D.S. al Fine

LIVE AND LET DIE

from LIVE AND LET DIE

ALTO SAX

Words and Music by PAUL McCARTNEY
and LINDA McCARTNEY

THE LOOK OF LOVE

from CASINO ROYALE

ALTO SAX

Words by HAL DAVID
Music by BURT BACHARACH

LUCK BE A LADY

from GUYS AND DOLLS

ALTO SAX

By FRANK LOESSER

A MAN AND A WOMAN

(Un homme et une femme)

from A MAN AND A WOMAN

ALTO SAX

Original Words by PIERRE BAROUH
English Words by JERRY KELLER
Music by FRANCIS LAI

MANIAC

from the Paramount Picture FLASHDANCE

ALTO SAX

Words and Music by MICHAEL SEMBELLO
and DENNIS MATKOSKY

MISSION: IMPOSSIBLE THEME

from the Paramount Motion Picture MISSION: IMPOSSIBLE

ALTO SAX

By LALO SCHIFRIN

MRS. ROBINSON

from THE GRADUATE

ALTO SAX

Words and Music by
PAUL SIMON

MOON RIVER

from the Paramount Picture BREAKFAST AT TIFFANY'S

ALTO SAX

Words by JOHNNY MERCER
Music by HENRY MANCINI

MORE

(Ti guarderò nel cuore)

from the film MONDO CANE

ALTO SAX

Music by NINO OLIVIERO and RIZ ORTOLANI
Italian Lyrics by MARCELLO CIORCIOLINI
English Lyrics by NORMAN NEWELL

THE MUSIC OF GOODBYE

from OUT OF AFRICA

ALTO SAX

Words and Music by JOHN BARRY,
ALAN BERGMAN and MARILYN BERGMAN

Moderately

MY HEART WILL GO ON

(Love Theme from 'Titanic')

from the Paramount and Twentieth Century Fox Motion Picture TITANIC

ALTO SAX

Music by JAMES HORNER
Lyric by WILL JENNINGS

NINE TO FIVE

from NINE TO FIVE

ALTO SAX

Words and Music by
DOLLY PARTON

NOTHING'S GONNA STOP US NOW

featured in MANNEQUIN

ALTO SAX

Words and Music by DIANE WARREN
and ALBERT HAMMOND

Moderate Rock

1.
2.

OLD TIME ROCK & ROLL

featured in RISKY BUSINESS

ALTO SAX

Words and Music by GEORGE JACKSON
and THOMAS E. JONES III

Medium Rock

THE PINK PANTHER

from THE PINK PANTHER

ALTO SAX

By HENRY MANCINI

PUT YOUR DREAMS AWAY (FOR ANOTHER DAY)

featured in INSIDE MOVES

ALTO SAX

Words by RUTH LOWE
Music by STEPHAN WEISS
and PAUL MANN

PUTTIN' ON THE RITZ

from the Motion Picture PUTTIN' ON THE RITZ

ALTO SAX

Words and Music by
IRVING BERLIN

Moderately, in 2

QUE SERA, SERA
(Whatever Will Be, Will Be)
from THE MAN WHO KNEW TOO MUCH

ALTO SAX

Words and Music by JAY LIVINGSTON
and RAYMOND B. EVANS

THE RAINBOW CONNECTION

from THE MUPPET MOVIE

ALTO SAX

Words and Music by PAUL WILLIAMS
and KENNETH L. ASCHER

RAINDROPS KEEP FALLIN' ON MY HEAD

from BUTCH CASSIDY AND THE SUNDANCE KID

ALTO SAX

Lyrics by HAL DAVID
Music by BURT BACHARACH

ROCK AROUND THE CLOCK

featured in the Motion Picture BLACKBOARD JUNGLE

ALTO SAX

Words and Music by MAX C. FREEDMAN
and JIMMY DeKNIGHT

LOVE THEME FROM "ST. ELMO'S FIRE"

from the Motion Picture ST. ELMO'S FIRE

ALTO SAX

Words and Music by
DAVID FOSTER

SAY YOU, SAY ME

from the Motion Picture WHITE NIGHTS

ALTO SAX

Words and Music by
LIONEL RICHIE

SEPARATE LIVES

Love Theme from WHITE NIGHTS

ALTO SAX

Words and Music by
STEPHEN BISHOP

Freely

THE SHADOW OF YOUR SMILE

Love Theme from THE SANDPIPER

ALTO SAX

Music by JOHNNY MANDEL
Words by PAUL FRANCIS WEBSTER

SOMEWHERE IN TIME

from SOMEWHERE IN TIME

ALTO SAX

By JOHN BARRY

SKYFALL

from the Motion Picture SKYFALL

ALTO SAX

Words and Music by ADELE ADKINS
and PAUL EPWORTH

3
3
D.S. al Coda
CODA
3

SOMEWHERE, MY LOVE

Lara's Theme from DOCTOR ZHIVAGO

ALTO SAX

Lyric by PAUL FRANCIS WEBSTER
Music by MAURICE JARRE

SOMEWHERE OUT THERE

from AN AMERICAN TAIL

ALTO SAX

Music by BARRY MANN and JAMES HORNER
Lyric by CYNTHIA WEIL

THE SOUND OF MUSIC

from THE SOUND OF MUSIC

ALTO SAX

Lyrics by OSCAR HAMMERSTEIN II
Music by RICHARD RODGERS

With much expression
To Coda
D.S. al Coda
CODA

SPEAK SOFTLY, LOVE

(Love Theme)

from the Paramount Picture THE GODFATHER

ALTO SAX

Words by LARRY KUSIK
Music by NINO ROTA

STAR TREK® THE MOTION PICTURE

Theme from the Paramount Picture STAR TREK: THE MOTION PICTURE

ALTO SAX

Music by
JERRY GOLDSMITH

Moderately fast March

SUMMER NIGHTS

from GREASE

ALTO SAX

Lyric and Music by WARREN CASEY
and JIM JACOBS

STAYIN' ALIVE

from the Motion Picture SATURDAY NIGHT FEVER

ALTO SAX

Words and Music by BARRY GIBB,
ROBIN GIBB and MAURICE GIBB

1.
2.

THE SWEETHEART TREE

from THE GREAT RACE

ALTO SAX

Words by JOHNNY MERCER
Music by HENRY MANCINI

Waltz tempo

SWINGING ON A STAR

from GOING MY WAY

ALTO SAX

Words by JOHNNY BURKE
Music by JIMMY VAN HEUSEN

Bright Swing

TAKE MY BREATH AWAY

(Love Theme)

from the Paramount Picture TOP GUN

ALTO SAX

Words and Music by GIORGIO MORODER
and TOM WHITLOCK

Moderately

2.

TAMMY

from TAMMY AND THE BACHELOR

ALTO SAX

Words and Music by JAY LIVINGSTON
and RAY EVANS

Moderately

THANKS FOR THE MEMORY

from the Paramount Picture BIG BROADCAST OF 1938

ALTO SAX

Words and Music by LEO ROBIN
and RALPH RAINGER

THAT'S AMORÉ
(That's Love)

from the Paramount Picture THE CADDY

ALTO SAX

Words by JACK BROOKS
Music by HARRY WARREN

A TIME FOR US

(Love Theme)

from the Paramount Picture ROMEO AND JULIET

ALTO SAX

Words by LARRY KUSIK
and EDDIE SNYDER
Music by NINO ROTA

TIME WARP

from THE ROCKY HORROR PICTURE SHOW

ALTO SAX

Words and Music by
RICHARD O'BRIEN

Moderately fast Rock

To Coda
Fine
D.S. al Coda
CODA
D.S.S. al Fine

TO SIR, WITH LOVE

from TO SIR, WITH LOVE

ALTO SAX

Words by DON BLACK
Music by MARC LONDON

UNCHAINED MELODY

from the Motion Picture UNCHAINED

ALTO SAX

Lyric by HY ZARET
Music by ALEX NORTH

TWO HEARTS
from BUSTER

ALTO SAX

Words and Music by PHIL COLLINS
and LAMONT DOZIER

Fast Swing

1.
2.
3
Fine
D.S. al Fine
(take 2nd ending)

UP WHERE WE BELONG

from the Paramount Picture AN OFFICER AND A GENTLEMAN

ALTO SAX

Words by WILL JENNINGS
Music by BUFFY SAINTE-MARIE and JACK NITZSCHE

THE WAY WE WERE

from the Motion Picture THE WAY WE WERE

ALTO SAX

Words by ALAN and MARILYN BERGMAN
Music by MARVIN HAMLISCH

WHEN SHE LOVED ME

from Walt Disney Pictures' TOY STORY 2 - A Pixar Film

ALTO SAX

Music and Lyrics by
RANDY NEWMAN

Slowly and freely

WHEN YOU BELIEVE
(From The Prince of Egypt)
from THE PRINCE OF EGYPT

ALTO SAX

Words and Music by
STEPHEN SCHWARTZ

WHEN YOU WISH UPON A STAR

from Walt Disney's PINOCCHIO

ALTO SAX

Words by NED WASHINGTON
Music by LEIGH HARLINE

WHERE DO I BEGIN

(Love Theme)

from the Paramount Picture LOVE STORY

ALTO SAX

Words by CARL SIGMAN
Music by FRANCIS LAI

WRITING'S ON THE WALL

from the film SPECTRE

ALTO SAX

Words and Music by SAM SMITH
and JAMES NAPIER

YOU LIGHT UP MY LIFE

from YOU LIGHT UP MY LIFE

ALTO SAX

Words and Music by
JOSEPH BROOKS

YOU MUST LOVE ME

from the Cinergi Motion Picture EVITA

ALTO SAX

Words by TIM RICE
Music by ANDREW LLOYD WEBBER

Moderately

HAL•LEONARD INSTRUMENTAL PLAY-ALONG

Your favorite songs are arranged just for solo instrumentalists with this outstanding series. Each book includes great full-accompaniment play-along audio so you can sound just like a pro!

Check out **halleonard.com** for songlists and more titles!

12 Pop Hits
12 songs
00261790 Flute · 00261795 Horn
00261791 Clarinet · 00261796 Trombone
00261792 Alto Sax · 00261797 Violin
00261793 Tenor Sax · 00261798 Viola
00261794 Trumpet · 00261799 Cello

The Very Best of Bach
15 selections
00225371 Flute · 00225376 Horn
00225372 Clarinet · 00225377 Trombone
00225373 Alto Sax · 00225378 Violin
00225374 Tenor Sax · 00225379 Viola
00225375 Trumpet · 00225380 Cello

The Beatles
15 songs
00225330 Flute · 00225335 Horn
00225331 Clarinet · 00225336 Trombone
00225332 Alto Sax · 00225337 Violin
00225333 Tenor Sax · 00225338 Viola
00225334 Trumpet · 00225339 Cello

Chart Hits
12 songs
00146207 Flute · 00146212 Horn
00146208 Clarinet · 00146213 Trombone
00146209 Alto Sax · 00146214 Violin
00146210 Tenor Sax · 00146211 Trumpet
00146216 Cello

Christmas Songs
12 songs
00146855 Flute · 00146863 Horn
00146858 Clarinet · 00146864 Trombone
00146859 Alto Sax · 00146866 Violin
00146860 Tenor Sax · 00146867 Viola
00146862 Trumpet · 00146868 Cello

Contemporary Broadway
15 songs
00298704 Flute · 00298709 Horn
00298705 Clarinet · 00298710 Trombone
00298706 Alto Sax · 00298711 Violin
00298707 Tenor Sax · 00298712 Viola
00298708 Trumpet · 00298713 Cello

Disney Movie Hits
12 songs
00841420 Flute · 00841424 Horn
00841687 Oboe · 00841425 Trombone
00841421 Clarinet · 00841426 Violin
00841422 Alto Sax · 00841427 Viola
00841686 Tenor Sax · 00841428 Cello
00841423 Trumpet

Prices, contents, and availability subject to change without notice.

Disney characters and artwork ™ & © 2021 Disney

Disney Solos
12 songs
00841404 Flute · 00841506 Oboe
00841406 Alto Sax · 00841409 Trumpet
00841407 Horn · 00841410 Violin
00841411 Viola · 00841412 Cello
00841405 Clarinet/Tenor Sax
00841408 Trombone/Baritone
00841553 Mallet Percussion

Dixieland Favorites
15 songs
00268756 Flute · 0068759 Trumpet
00268757 Clarinet · 00268760 Trombone
00268758 Alto Sax

Billie Eilish
9 songs
00345648 Flute · 00345653 Horn
00345649 Clarinet · 00345654 Trombone
00345650 Alto Sax · 00345655 Violin
00345651 Tenor Sax · 00345656 Viola
00345652 Trumpet · 00345657 Cello

Favorite Movie Themes
13 songs
00841166 Flute · 00841168 Trumpet
00841167 Clarinet · 00841170 Trombone
00841169 Alto Sax · 00841296 Violin

Gospel Hymns
15 songs
00194648 Flute · 00194654 Trombone
00194649 Clarinet · 00194655 Violin
00194650 Alto Sax · 00194656 Viola
00194651 Tenor Sax · 00194657 Cello
00194652 Trumpet

Great Classical Themes
15 songs
00292727 Flute · 00292733 Horn
00292728 Clarinet · 00292735 Trombone
00292729 Alto Sax · 00292736 Violin
00292730 Tenor Sax · 00292737 Viola
00292732 Trumpet · 00292738 Cello

The Greatest Showman
8 songs
00277389 Flute · 00277394 Horn
00277390 Clarinet · 00277395 Trombone
00277391 Alto Sax · 00277396 Violin
00277392 Tenor Sax · 00277397 Viola
00277393 Trumpet · 00277398 Cello

Irish Favorites
31 songs
00842489 Flute · 00842495 Trombone
00842490 Clarinet · 00842496 Violin
00842491 Alto Sax · 00842497 Viola
00842493 Trumpet · 00842498 Cello
00842494 Horn

Michael Jackson
11 songs
00119495 Flute · 00119499 Trumpet
00119496 Clarinet · 00119501 Trombone
00119497 Alto Sax · 00119503 Violin
00119498 Tenor Sax · 00119502 Accomp.

Jazz & Blues
14 songs
00841438 Flute · 00841441 Trumpet
00841439 Clarinet · 00841443 Trombone
00841440 Alto Sax · 00841444 Violin
00841442 Tenor Sax

Jazz Classics
12 songs
00151812 Flute · 00151816 Trumpet
00151813 Clarinet · 00151818 Trombone
00151814 Alto Sax · 00151819 Violin
00151815 Tenor Sax · 00151821 Cello

Les Misérables
13 songs
00842292 Flute · 00842297 Horn
00842293 Clarinet · 00842298 Trombone
00842294 Alto Sax · 00842299 Violin
00842295 Tenor Sax · 00842300 Viola
00842296 Trumpet · 00842301 Cello

Metallica
12 songs
02501327 Flute · 02502454 Horn
02501339 Clarinet · 02501329 Trombone
02501332 Alto Sax · 02501334 Violin
02501333 Tenor Sax · 02501335 Viola
02501330 Trumpet · 02501338 Cello

Motown Classics
15 songs
00842572 Flute · 00842576 Trumpet
00842573 Clarinet · 00842578 Trombone
00842574 Alto Sax · 00842579 Violin
00842575 Tenor Sax

Pirates of the Caribbean
16 songs
00842183 Flute · 00842188 Horn
00842184 Clarinet · 00842189 Trombone
00842185 Alto Sax · 00842190 Violin
00842186 Tenor Sax · 00842191 Viola
00842187 Trumpet · 00842192 Cello

Queen
17 songs
00285402 Flute · 00285407 Horn
00285403 Clarinet · 00285408 Trombone
00285404 Alto Sax · 00285409 Violin
00285405 Tenor Sax · 00285410 Viola
00285406 Trumpet · 00285411 Cello

Simple Songs
14 songs
00249081 Flute · 00249087 Horn
00249093 Oboe · 00249089 Trombone
00249082 Clarinet · 00249090 Violin
00249083 Alto Sax · 00249091 Viola
00249084 Tenor Sax · 00249092 Cello
00249086 Trumpet · 00249094 Mallets

Superhero Themes
14 songs
00363195 Flute · 00363200 Horn
00363196 Clarinet · 00363201 Trombone
00363197 Alto Sax · 00363202 Violin
00363198 Tenor Sax · 00363203 Viola
00363199 Trumpet · 00363204 Cello

Star Wars
16 songs
00350900 Flute · 00350907 Horn
00350913 Oboe · 00350908 Trombone
00350903 Clarinet · 00350909 Violin
00350904 Alto Sax · 00350910 Viola
00350905 Tenor Sax · 00350911 Cello
00350906 Trumpet · 00350914 Mallet

Taylor Swift
15 songs
00842532 Flute · 00842537 Horn
00842533 Clarinet · 00842538 Trombone
00842534 Alto Sax · 00842539 Violin
00842535 Tenor Sax · 00842540 Viola
00842536 Trumpet · 00842541 Cello

Video Game Music
13 songs
00283877 Flute · 00283883 Horn
00283878 Clarinet · 00283884 Trombone
00283879 Alto Sax · 00283885 Violin
00283880 Tenor Sax · 00283886 Viola
00283882 Trumpet · 00283887 Cello

Wicked
13 songs
00842236 Flute · 00842241 Horn
00842237 Clarinet · 00842242 Trombone
00842238 Alto Sax · 00842243 Violin
00842239 Tenor Sax · 00842244 Viola
00842240 Trumpet · 00842245 Cello

HAL•LEONARD®

0122
488